EXTREME NATURE

WILD WEATHER

Anita Ganeri

Raintree

www.raintreepublishers.co.uk
Visit our website to find out
more information about
Raintree books.

To order:
☎ Phone 0845 6044371
📄 Fax +44 (0) 1865 312263
✉ Email myorders@raintreepublishers.co.uk

Customers from outside the UK please telephone +44 1865 312262

Raintree is an imprint of Capstone Global Library
Limited, a company incorporated in England and
Wales having its registered office at 7 Pilgrim Street,
London, EC4V 6LB – Registered company number:
6695582

Edited by Dan Nunn, Rebecca Rissman,
  and Catherine Veitch
Designed by Cynthia Della-Rovere
Picture research by Tracy Cummins
Production by Alison Parsons
Originated by Capstone Global Library
Printed and bound in China by CTPS

ISBN 978 1 406 23791 7
16 15 14 13 12
10 9 8 7 6 5 4 3 2 1

British Library Cataloguing in Publication Data
Ganeri, Anita
Wild weather. -- (Extreme nature)
551.5'5-dc22
A full catalogue record for this book is available from
the British Library.

Acknowledgements
We would like to thank the following for permission
to reproduce photographs: Alamy p. 27 (© AfriPics.
com); Corbis pp. 4 (© China Newsphoto/Reuters), 10
(© Eric Nguyen), 19 (© HAZIR REKA/Reuters), 22 (©
DLILLC), 23 (REUTERS/China Daily); Getty Images pp.
9 (Paul Katz), 12 (Mike Theiss), 15 (Jim Reed/Science
Faction), 16 (Laurent VAN DER STOCKT/Gamma-
Rapho), 17 (YURI CORTEZ/AFP), 18 (David Cannon),
21 (rolfo/Flickr), 24 (Jeremy Woodhouse), 25 (Alex
Wong); istockphoto pp. 7 (© David Parsons), 13 (©
Steve Shepard); National Oceanic and Atmospheric
Administration (NOAA) p. 14; Shutterstock pp. 5 (©
Stevacek), 6 (© pakowacz), 8 (© Vadim Subbotin), 11
(© R. Gino Santa Mari), 20 (© Sam Chadwick), 26 (©
Galyna Andrushko).

Cover photograph of winter reproduced with
permission of istockphoto (© Martyn Unsworth).
Background photograph of a dark sky with storm
clouds reproduced with permission of Shutterstock
(© pzAxe).

Every effort has been made to contact copyright
holders of material reproduced in this book. Any
omissions will be rectified in subsequent printings if
notice is given to the publisher.

Some words are shown in bold, **like this**. You can find
out what they mean by looking in the glossary.

Contents

What is wild weather?

Did you know that about 100 flashes of **lightning** hit Earth every second? Did you know that **tornadoes** are the world's strongest winds? Wild weather happens everywhere. You can find out more about it in this book.

Storm clouds gather over these fields.

Lightning is a spark of electricity. The electricity builds up inside a **thundercloud**. Suddenly, the electricity escapes as a giant spark. The spark jumps between the bottom of the cloud and the ground.

DID YOU KNOW?
A flash of lightning heats the air so quickly that the air makes a loud booming sound – thunder.

This tree has been struck by lightning.

Lightning usually takes the quickest path to the ground. Tall trees, buildings, and sometimes people can be hit.

8

Some buildings have **lightning conductors** on their roofs. These are metal rods that carry the electricity safely down to the ground.

lightning conductor

DID YOU KNOW?
Unlucky Roy Sullivan from the United States was struck by lightning seven times!

Twisting tornadoes

Tornadoes are spinning twists of wind that race across land. They start in **thunderclouds**, then they spin down to the ground.

DID YOU KNOW?
In 1931, a tornado in the United States lifted a whole train into the air.

Tornadoes can destroy buildings. They can suck up cars and carry them through the air.

Tornado Alley, in the Midwest of the United States, has about 700 tornadoes every year. In 2011, a huge tornado hit the city of Joplin, Missouri. Over 130 people died, and hundreds more were injured. Thousands of homes were destroyed.

SAFE
SHELTER

Many people living in
Tornado Alley have
underground storm shelters.
These are safe places to
hide when a tornado strikes.

13

Horrible hurricanes

Hurricanes are like giant spinning wheels of clouds, wind, and rain. Strangely, there is a small, circular area in the middle of a hurricane where the weather is calm and clear. It is called the "eye".

eye

DID YOU KNOW?
A hurricane can be enormous – about 500 kilometres across. That is about half the length of Great Britain!

New Orleans,
United States

Hurricanes start over the sea, then often blow across land. In August 2005, Hurricane Katrina hit the southern coast of the United States. It damaged many cities and towns, and killed more than 1,800 people.

DID YOU KNOW?
Hurricanes are given names from an alphabetical list. David, Tracey, and Andrew were particularly fierce ones.

Hammering hail

A **hailstone** is a ball of hard ice that falls from a **thundercloud**. Hailstones are usually pea-sized, but they can be much bigger. Sometimes, hailstones are big enough to flatten farmers' crops, smash windows, and even hurt people.

DID YOU KNOW?

In 1970, a hailstone as big as a melon fell in Kansas, USA!

Hailstones flattened this crop of tomatoes in Kosovo, in Europe.

Blinding blizzards

A **blizzard** is a snowstorm. It has heavy snow, icy winds, and freezing cold temperatures. Blizzards can be deadly. They can bury cars, lorries, and trains under snow.

The snow makes it difficult for people to walk or drive.

DID YOU KNOW?
The worst kind of blizzard is called a "white-out". It is difficult to see anything in a "white-out".

Forceful floods

Most floods happen when storms bring heavy rain. The rain makes rivers burst their banks, and water flows on to the land. Flood water can wash away buildings, roads, crops, animals, and people. Weather stations send out **flood alerts** to warn people to get ready for floods.

This man is trying to stop the flood water from coming into his home.

Baking heatwaves

A **heatwave** is a long stretch of very hot weather. It usually lasts for about three days.

People can get heatstroke in a heatwave. They feel sick and dizzy. It is important to keep cool and to drink lots of water.

Dreadful droughts

A **drought** happens when a place gets much less rain than usual. Lakes and rivers dry up. Crops cannot grow without water. People and animals do not have water to drink or food to eat.

In a drought, the soil may turn to dust and cause dust storms.

Quiz: What am I?

Read the clues, then try to work out "What am I?". Find the answers at the bottom of page 29. But guess first!

1) I am a giant spark.
I start in a **thundercloud**.
I jump to the ground.
What am I?

2) I spin around and around.
I race across the ground.
I can destroy buildings.
What am I?

3) I have an "eye".
I can be 500 kilometres across.
I start over the sea.
What am I?

4) I am made of ice.
I can be as big as a melon.
I fall from a thundercloud.
What am I?

5) I am very hot.
I can last for several days.
I can make people ill.
What am I?

Answers: **1)** lightning **2)** tornado **3)** hurricane
4) hailstone **5)** heatwave.

Glossary

blizzard severe snowstorm

drought time of very dry weather when there is very little or no rain

dust storm storm with strong winds and swirling dust

flood alert warning given to people to tell them that floods are likely

hailstone ball of hard ice that falls from a thundercloud

heatwave stretch of very hot weather

hurricane giant spinning storm

lightning giant spark of electricity that builds up inside a thundercloud

lightning conductor metal rod that catches lightning and carries it down safely to the ground

thundercloud huge black cloud. It is called a cumulonimbus cloud.

tornado violently spinning twist of wind

Find out more

Books

Graphic Natural Disasters series
(Franklin Watts, 2010)

Wild Weather series, Catherine Chambers
(Raintree Publishing, 2007)

Websites

teacher.scholastic.com/activities/wwatch

Track some stormy weather and find out more about what makes the weather turn wild with this interactive website.

www.bbc.co.uk/schools/whatisweather

This interactive BBC website introduces you to all kinds of weather, and how people live with it.

Index